A Lexicon of Practical Terms for Pet Consultants!

The language You Need

Published by DogNostics Career Center

This Lexicon lists ethological, behavior analytic, pet cognition, neuroaffective, neurobiological, psychological and common terms, in an attempt to provide a complete understanding of pet behavior terminology, to assist professionals and students of behavior.

Original publication 2012. Contributed to by Niki Tudge, Louise Stapleton-Frappell & Angelica Steinker.

Updated August 2018 by Niki Tudge and Louise Stapleton-Frappell

Third Edition – September 2018.

Table of Contents

A

Ability

What an individual pet has the potential to accomplish. Ex. A pet that is not motivated to run an agility course may do so very slowly although she has the skills, is healthy mentally and physically, to run it very quickly.

Abuse

A non-accidental physical or emotional injury committed by a person toward a pet. Abuse generally results in physical pain and/or post-traumatic stress disorder.

Accountability

The acknowledgement and acceptance of the responsibilities we have to our industry, our clients and our peers in terms of our training and how we conduct ourselves in business.

Acquisition

Acquisition is the first stage of learning a new skill where a response is evoked and selected for reinforcement.

Active Student Responding

What behavior consultants aim for when instructing clients. As people trainers we need to be sure that clients can display and provide evidence that they understand and can competently complete the mechanical skills required to train their pet.

Activity Reinforcer

Also called the Premack Principle or Premack Reinforcer. Pets are given access to a more highly reinforcing activity after performing a less reinforcing activity. Ex. A pet is released to run and play in the back yard after they perform a sit and wait at the door prior to it being opened.   This makes the target behavior of sitting and waiting more likely because of the reinforcement contingency of being released to run and play.

Affect

A feeling, which can be inferred in a pet by outward expressions of posture, facial expression and movements consistent with that pet's individual ethogram. Affect, along with motivation and cognition, create what is called a triad of psychological functions which is associated with the mammalian limbic system.

Affective Aggression

Affective Aggression provokes the sympathetic nervous system, emotional arousal. It is very different to non-affective aggression, predation.

Aggression

Aggressive behaviors are the onset of a coercive or destructive process, and threat. Aggressive operants are growling, snarling, snapping and lunges or bites. Aggressive behaviors are operant behaviors and are reinforced through their consequences. Pets learn that by using aggressive behaviors they can access pleasant stimulus or avoid or escape aversive stimulus.

Anthropomorphism

The projection of human characteristics onto a pet. Ex. when I returned home my dog looked guilty because they had soiled in the home and they knew this would disappoint me!

Antecedent

A stimulus that precedes in order the behavior that directly follows it. The antecedent happens immediately before the behavior and in Operant Conditioning it is responsible for evoking the behavior whereas in Respondent Conditioning we say the antecedent elicits the behavior. The antecedent package includes the distance antecedents (setting events & motivating operations) as well as the direct antecedent, the discriminative stimulus or conditioned stimulus.

Anecdotal evidence

First or second-hand information about an individual's personal experience. Both positive and negative anecdotal evidence are unreliable as they do not provide tangible data that can be stratified, analyzed or scientifically interpreted.

Antecedent Control

The management and anticipation of a response to an eliciting or evoking stimulus. By changing the relationship through effectively altering the predictive stimulus or response to the stimulus. (Any behavioral intervention is far more complex than what can be summarized in a paragraph.)

Applied Behavior Analysis

A science that uses behavior principles to solve practical problems

Amygdala

A small structure in the mammalian brain that is important to the limbic system which is involved in emotions such as anger, fear and freezing.

Appetitive Stimulus

An Appetitive Stimulus is a reinforcing stimulus. It is something the pet finds positively reinforcing. Please note the pet, not the trainer determines what is positively reinforcing. A reinforcer is only a reinforcer in relation to a specific behavior, in a specific context and with a particular individual.

Approximation

When a behavior is trained in separate pieces, each component part of the final behavior is called an approximation. Each approximation that leads us closer to the goal behavior is reinforced.

Association

The conditioning process that links one stimulus with another stimulus.

Attention Seeking Behavior

Any behavior that a trainer has determined through the process of conducting a functional analysis is purposed to achieve attention.

Autonomic Nervous System

The part of the nervous system that regulates activity of the internal organs which includes the sympathetic and parasympathetic nervous systems.

AutoShaping

A type of conditioning in which the conditioned response has neither been directly reinforced nor punished but is instead a modified instinctive response to the environment.

Aversive

Any stimulus that a pet attempts to escape or avoid is considered an aversive. The addition of an aversive serves as a positive punisher and the removal of an aversive serves as a negative reinforcer.

Avoidance

A behavior that functions to allow the pet to avoid something unpleasant. Escape and avoidance behaviors are negatively reinforced. Ideal training situations exclude the strategic use of aversives that drive avoidance. Accidental negative reinforcement is unavoidable in real life, but training protocols should not be built on negative reinforcement.

B

Backward Chaining

Where you teach a task by teaching the last step of the chain first. Chaining is an appropriate procedure to employ when training a sequence of behaviors, two or more component behaviors that will be performed in a sequence, with one cue used to evoke the final behavior. In contrast to forward chaining, in backward chaining the trainer chooses to start with the last part of the behavior first. Backwards Chaining is often preferred to Forwards Chaining as the pet drives towards the final known behavior in the chain to receive reinforcement

Backward Conditioning

One of the four ways conditioning takes place in Respondent Conditioning. Backward conditioning presents the unconditioned stimulus before the conditioned stimulus and weakens the contingency between the conditioned stimulus and the unconditioned stimulus. In respondent conditioning the amount of learning depends on the degree to which the conditioned stimulus predicts the unconditioned stimulus.

Baseline

The baseline is the frequency, duration, intensity, latency of the skill/behavior observed prior to any intervention. Baseline measures are used as a starting point to a training plan. Having a baseline measure allows the trainer to be sure that any behavior plan or training plan is having the correct impact on the behavior as progression or regression can be quickly identified.

Behavior

Behavior is anything a pet does that can be observed and measured. Behaviors are voluntary or involuntary reactions or actions to the individual's environment. Behavior is the output of the relationship between the pet and their environment. It is also suggested that behavior can also include thoughts but as behavior analysts we cannot see or witness this.

Behaviorism

The theory that pet behavior can be explained in terms of conditioning, without any consideration given to thoughts or feelings and other disorders.

Behavior Blindness

The trainer does not pay attention to the emotional response or operant behavior of a pet as they are too focused on the delivery of a specific goal behavior.

Behavior Chain

A compound linear chain consists of a series of component behaviors performed in sequence. The final behavior chain is often placed under stimulus control of a compound cue. A retrieve is a good example of a behavior chain.

Behavioral Deficit

When a pet cannot perform a behavior that it should be able to perform at its age, because it lacks the skills.

Behavior Goal

The behavior goal is the required end result of the training or behavior change program. In client consulting, this is driven by the needs of the client versus the reality of the pet's age, emotional needs and living conditions.

Behavior Modification

The process by which pet behavior consultants change problematic or undesirable behaviors.

Behavior Modification/Change Plan

A written plan that outlines what the pet behavior consultant is recommending to the client to facilitate the modification of the pet's behavior. A good behavior treatment plan is detailed and is followed up on to track effectiveness.

Behavior Patterns

A predictable pattern of behavior that is life stage limited or life course persistent which can include patterns of attachment, aggression, learning, sexuality, addiction or communication.

Behavior System

Konrad Lorenz coined the term *behavior systems* as a replacement for the term instinct. *Behavior system* describes behaviors that are linked together and that appear to be innate. Also called fixed action patterns and, more currently, modal action patterns.

Behavior Trap

Can also be referred to as self-reinforcing behavior. For example, many pets find barking intrinsically reinforcing - Barking does not require any external reinforcement (food, attention or play) and is thus promoted and maintained.

Behavioral Economics

The phenomenon for pets to develop strategies of getting the most amount of food for the least amount of work.

Behavioral Momentum

The tendency for a behavior to become more resistant to extinction the greater it's reinforcement history.

Bite Inhibition

A process through which, as the result of play and appropriate socialization, domesticated pets learn to inhibit hard biting. For example: Having learned bite inhibition, the seven-month-old puppy no longer mouths the human petting her.

Blocking also called Blocking Effect

A Respondent Conditioning phenomenon when a pet fails to learn an association with a stimulus as a result of it being presented at the same time with an already learned stimulus that is more powerful. Blocking is not the same as overshadowing which applies to operant conditioning.

Block of Trials

The total number of attempts, trials, when teaching a pet or client a new behavior.

Bribery

The giving of reinforcement prior to a pet performing a behavior. Poor training uses food prior to obtaining behavior, stimulus control or proper lure fading. This often results in the pet not carrying out the behavior if the bribe is not present. This is not a reflection of using food in training, this is the result of inadequate training and mechanical skills.

Bridge or Bridging

A stimulus that spans the time gap between the behavior and the delivery of the reinforcer. The clicker is a bridge. Using a verbal "yes" marker, is also a bridge.

C

Capturing

A training process which makes use of reinforcing a behavior as it is observed. To effectively capture a behavior, we need to recognize the existing antecedents to said behavior so that we can reliably predict when the behavior will occur.

Case Study

A description of the history and behavior modification of a particular pet by journaling improvements, setbacks and the processes used. Case study information may suffer from bias and inaccuracies which is why the scientific method is ideal. A case study is NOT a single subject experimental design (which is a scientific procedure). It should be noted that case studies can be extremely persuasive which is why it is so important for pet behavior consultants to be able to substantiate their training and recommendations using learning and behavior principles.

Catharsis

A psychological mechanism by which punishing a human or pet can become positively reinforcing. Also called abreaction, this mechanism occurs when one being redirects aggression on another, which consequently is negatively reinforcing to the aggressor and positively punishing to the victim. It is important to be aware that all humans are capable of experiencing catharsis and that this is always harmful to both parties. Losing your temper and yelling at a human or pet is a form of catharsis.

Chaining

See Behavior Chain

Choice

Providing more than one scenario for a pet to choose from. Giving pets and humans choices empowers them to choose to comply rather than forcing them to comply which sets them up for more ideal learning that is less stressful and more fun. Empowerment training keeps the emphasis on the emotional state of the pet, reinforcing behaviors consistent with fun, joy and play.

Circadian Rhythm

A cycle of physiological changes in behavior linked to the 24-hour cycle of our days. Ex. Every day at 5pm the puppy gets the "zoomies" and races around the house.

Classical Conditioning

Also called Respondent Conditioning or Pavlovian Conditioning, deals with reflexive behaviors and emotions. Respondent Conditioning takes place when an unconditioned stimulus that elicits an unconditioned response is repeatedly paired with a neutral stimulus. As a result of conditioning, the neutral stimulus becomes a conditioned stimulus that reliably elicits a conditioned response. Each single pairing is considered a trial. With respondent conditioning, the two stimuli, neutral and unconditioned, are presented regardless of the behavior the individual is exhibiting. The behavior elicited is a reflex response.

Classical Counterconditioning

Also called respondent counterconditioning. A training process that modifies undesired associations (fear) by replacing it with desired associations (joy). This is the procedure used to change a problematic emotional response to a relaxed or happy response.

Clickerwise

Common term referring to a pet that has learned the concepts of luring, capturing, and shaping thus being able to learn at a more rapid rate than a pet that is not "clickerwise". Arousal or stress can interfere with a pet's ability to be "clickerwise".

Closed Economy

A training procedure requiring the pet to work for all reinforcement. In a closed economy a pet would not be fed from a food bowl. All resources would only be available during training sessions.

Coercion

The use or threat of punishment to intimidate a pet into a specific behavior by then removing the threat or punishment when they comply. The functioning of positive punishment and negative reinforcement.

Coercive Procedures

Any procedure that makes use of force or threats is considered to be coercive.

Cognition

A pet's attending to, identifying, categorizing or acting upon information obtained from the environment or internal setting events. The mental processes used to acquire, organize and apply information.

Command

A word used to describe a cue. Not commonly used in the positive reinforcement community as it connotates a "do or else" approach to training.

Commitment Point

The commitment point is, based on the individual pet's ethogram, the moment the pet has made the decision to perform the specific behavior you are working on. Ex. If recalling, the moment the pet snaps his head back toward you. Marking and reinforcing commitment can make for clearer learning and a faster training process.

Competing Behavior

A behavior that interferes with the teaching of a new skill or makes it difficult to target the new behavior for reinforcement.

Compliance Mindset

When training using compulsion, traditional, force training, the pet is not given a choice. As a result, the trainer develops a compliance mindset. The trainer does not want to give the pet any choice.

Compulsive Training or Compulsion Training

Training that, through an approach or choice of tools and equipment, provides aversives to evoke behavior.

Conditioned Emotional Response

Abbreviation: CER. A negative conditioned emotional response occurs when a previously neutral stimulus is paired with an aversive unconditioned stimulus, resulting in the neutral stimulus eliciting a fear (conditioned) response. A positive conditioned emotional response occurs when a previously neutral stimulus is paired with an appetitive unconditioned stimulus.

Conditioned Negative Punisher

Also known as no reward marker or non-reward marker. A stimulus, such as a word or phrase, that is-linked with negative punishment via associative learning. Ex. The pet performs an unwanted behavior. The trainer says: "too bad" and places the pet in time out. "Too bad" predicts time out for the pet.

Conditioned Negative Reinforcer

A stimulus, such as a sound or word, that acquires reinforcing properties as a result of being associated with the withdrawal of an aversive stimulus. Ex. A leashed pet darts out ahead of the handler, the handler says "no" and then begins yanking on the leash repeatedly until the pet falls into heel position next to the handler.

Conditioned Punisher

A previously neutral stimulus that takes on punishing properties because of repeated pairing with punishment. Ex. The beeping sound of the invisible fence signals to the pet that a shock is about to occur. The beep becomes a conditioned positive punisher.

Conditioned Reinforcer

Anything which was not previously reinforcing that has taken on positively reinforcing properties is a conditioned positive reinforcer.

The sound of the clicker is a conditioned reinforcer.

Conditioned Response

A conditioned response is a learned response to a given set of conditions occurring in the environment.

Conditioned Stimulus.

As a result of conditioning, the neutral stimulus (a leash) becomes a conditioned stimulus (predicative of going for a walk) that reliably elicits a conditioned response.

Conditioning

Respondent conditioning involves the pairing of stimuli. There are four ways of pairing the unconditioned stimulus and conditioned stimulus. The rate of respondent conditioning will vary with the degree of CS – US contingency. The interval, contiguity, between the conditioned stimulus and unconditioned stimulus also affects how quickly conditioning occurs. Trace and delayed conditioning present the conditioned stimulus prior to the unconditioned stimulus. In simultaneous conditioning and backward conditioning, the conditioned stimulus is not presented before the unconditioned stimulus but either simultaneously or after the unconditioned stimulus is presented.

Conditioned Reflex

A conditioned reflex occurs when a conditioned stimulus (CS) creates a conditioned response (CR). This is a learned response to a given set of conditions occurring in the environment. Pavlov recognized that any stimulus could become a conditioned stimulus when paired repeatedly with an unconditioned stimulus.

Conditioned Reinforcers

Conditioned reinforcers, referred to as secondary reinforcers, are dependent on an association with other reinforcers. They owe their effectiveness directly or indirectly to primary reinforcers.

Confirmation Bias

A bias for or against certain information to confirm one's beliefs. Ex. Every pet I have ever spanked with a rolled-up newspaper became housetrained so obviously this method works.

Confound

A confound is a variable that influences the relationship between two other variables. We can mistakenly draw a conclusion about the relationship between two variables being studied, when we fail to eliminate a third, confounding variable that is influencing those variables. Ex. The pet eats a potato. The pet vomits. Conclusion: Potatoes cause a pet to vomit. There is a confounding variable that has not been considered. The pet had eaten some garbage prior to eating the potato

Consequence

A consequence is a postcedent, it occurs after the behavior and is a reinforcing factor to the preceding behavior. The quadrant of operant conditioning describes the four possible results that can strengthen or weaken a behavior and thus are consequences. Positive reinforcement, Negative reinforcement, Positive punishment and negative punishment are the four learning mechanisms that constitute the consequences. In a functional analysis the antecedent, behavior and consequence are analyzed.

Operant conditioning follows an ABC formula. Antecedent → Behavior → Consequence. (Cue → behavior → consequence).

Consent Test

By evaluating a pet's emotions via their social communication system, we enable and empower them to walk away or stay and engage in an activity we are performing.

Contiguity

The proximity, or temporal relationship, between the stimulus and the response

Continuation Bridge

See Keep Going Signal.

Contra-Free Loading

When offered a choice between free food and working for food, the pet chooses to work for the food. Current research shows that self-reinforcement and the obligatory species-specific response hypothesis are not enough to explain these phenomena.

Cortisol

A hormone manufactured by the adrenal glands which is linked to stress. Forceful training increases levels of cortisol thus it is not recommended.

Countercondition or Counterconditioning

Counter conditioning works alongside a graded desensitization plan. During the counter conditioning component of the systematic desensitization there must be a contrast between the "open bar" process of the systematic desensitization and the "closed bar". When the fear eliciting stimulus is presented, all great things happen, and they are quickly removed with the exit of the fear eliciting stimulus. There must be both a temporal relationship and a contingency between the conditioned stimulus and the unconditioned stimulus for conditioning to occur and for the problematic emotional response to be replaced with a new more appropriate response.

Contingency

Contingency is an if/then then scenario. It describes the cause and effect between the behavior and the consequence.

Contingent Observation

Social learning can occur if one pet is placed in a time out while being able to observe another pet performing the desired behavior. If you put one of your pets in a crate and, in view of the crated pet, you perform the behavior and play with the second pet, the crated pet is experiencing contingent observation. (Behavior analysts typically call this an inclusionary time out.)

Contingency Statement

A contingency statement is an if/then statement. The statement describes the cause and effect relationship between the antecedent and behavior or behavior and its consequences. Y is contingent on X. Y is the dependent variable of X. Therefore, X would either be the antecedent or the consequence in a contingency statement about behavior.

Continuity

The period of time delay that occurs prior to commencement of the reinforcement process. t. Ex. Click, three second pause, then treat. Excessive continuity may result in pets producing superstitious behaviors.

Continuous Reinforcement (CRF)

A Fixed Schedule 1:1. One of many schedules of reinforcement where the pet is reinforced every single time the behavior is performed. This creates a very reliable performance but also one dependent on the reinforcer, thus this schedule of reinforcement can be prone to extinction. Continuous reinforcement is NOT a recommended schedule of reinforcement in the maintenance stage as it creates a psychological dependency on the reinforcement. However, when a behavior is in early acquisition, you should reinforce every occurrence.

Correlation

Correlation is a scientific mechanism that establishes to what degree two things are positively or negatively connected. Positive correlation means both variables increase or decrease together. Negative correlation means that as one variable increases, the other decreases. Correlation is NOT causation. Ex. Increased income is connected to increased expenditure on pet care services.

Covert Behavior

Thoughts and feelings are considered covert behavior. In pet training covert behaviors are often accessible behaviorally by establishing and then reading the individual's signs of stress and signs of joy, creating individual ethograms. Even though covert behavior is a private event, it is subject to the same principles of learning as overt behavior.

Criteria

The characteristics or individual components of a behavioral response which the trainer determines will be marked and reinforced. Criteria should be clearly defined and appropriate for the individual learner, behavior and environment.

Criterion

Singular of Criteria

Cue

A request for a pet to perform a behavior. Cues are antecedents. See Discriminative Stimulus.

Curriculum

The behaviors that one is teaching comprise your curriculum. Could also be a bank of behaviors or material from which you choose what you will be teaching a given pet.

D

Data

Information that is scientifically gathered and analyzed to make ideal decisions about behavior modification programs.

Dead Person's Test

A mechanism of critical thinking used to determine if something is a behavior or not. If a dead person can do it, it isn't behavior. This test can be used in the creation of behavior goals and behavior modification plans.

Decision Point

See Commitment Point

Default Behavior

The behavior that has the highest likelihood of occurring; a preferred behavior. It could be the first behavior trained, or a behavior that is assumed to be enjoyable to the pet.

Delay Conditioning

One of the four ways conditioning takes place in Respondent Conditioning. With delayed conditioning there is an overlap of the conditioned stimulus and unconditioned stimulus. Delayed conditioning is also affected by the length of delay between the presentation of the conditioned stimulus and the unconditioned stimulus; these delays are referred to as short and long delays. In respondent conditioning the amount of learning depends on the degree to which the conditioned stimulus predicts the unconditioned stimulus. With both trace and delayed conditioning, a conditional response begins to appear after the conditioned stimulus is presented as there is a high degree of CS-US contingency and there is an interstimulus interval.

Delay of Reinforcement

Deferment of the positive reinforcer. Not ideal when a behavior is in acquisition and not yet under ideal stimulus control. Delay of reinforcement is used when a keep going signal is given, informing the pet they are on the right track, but that reinforcement is not yet coming.

Deprivation

Withholding or lack of something considered to be a basic necessity. Deprivation is comprised of both ethical and unethical deprivation. Starving a pet to lose a percentage of normal body weight, excessive social isolation, lack of environmental enrichment are all unethical forms of deprivation. Ethical deprivation is measuring a pet's full daily ration and using it to conduct training sessions (closed economy).

Desensitization

Presentation of a stimulus at a level of intensity that elicits little or no response from the pet, then gradually increasing the intensity of the stimulus (Karen Pryor). This is the process by which a fearful pet will get used to the bang of the teeter (seesaw), and the movement of the teeter, but only if the approximations are tiny and the training very gradual.

Discrimination

Discrimination training is the procedure used to establish discrimination between stimuli. In respondent conditioning a pet can be trained to discriminate and behave differently in two situations. The pet may respond to the CS^+ but not to the CS^-. With Operant conditioning one stimulus, S^D, indicates a behavior that will be reinforced, and the S^A indicates the behavior that will not be reinforced. Both S^D and S^A are discriminative stimuli. Discrimination occurs when one consequence is more reinforcing than another and the pet behaves differently in the situations. Difficult discriminations can be shaped by gradually making the stimulus (CS$^+$, CS$^-$ or S^D, S^A) more alike.

Differential Outcome Effect (DOE)

Discrimination occurs more quickly and/or more accurately when different behaviors are reinforced using unique reinforcers. Each discriminative stimulus-response is followed by a particular reinforcer. The pet not only forms an association between the S.D. and the response but also between the response and the reinforcer. This can be effective when working on inter-cue discrimination.

Differential Reinforcement of Excellent Behavior (DRE)

A schedule of reinforcement that is used by a trainer to reinforce more excellent (faster, minimal latency/high fluency performances). Pets are able to learn the pattern of DRE you are using. If you consistently reinforce for fast, minimal latency and accurate performances the pet will default to doing things quickly, with minimal latency and accurate.

Differential Reinforcement

Differential reinforcement is a procedure to help modify unwanted behaviors. Rather than working with just extinction which can create frustration, it is more effective to target the problem behavior for extinction while simultaneously reinforcing a more preferable behavior. There are several methods of differential reinforcement. Some of the more commonly used are **Differential Reinforcement** of Alternative Behavior (DRA), **Differential Reinforcement** of Other Behavior (DRO), **Differential Reinforcement** of Incompatible Behavior (DRI), **Differential Reinforcement** of High Rates of Behavior (DRH). Differential reinforcement focuses on desirable behaviors not undesirable behaviors.

Direct Observation

Direct Observation is the second component of a Functional Assessment. If necessary to establish an accurate contingency statement, the targeted behavior is observed and tracked so the relationship between the behavior, the antecedents and the consequences can be understood and professionally and systematically addressed through behavior change programs.

Discrimination

Refers to the pet's ability to differentiate between a conditioned stimulus and an unconditioned stimulus.

Discrimination Training

Any training process that requires the pet to discriminate is discrimination training. Teaching a pet the difference between the cues "tunnel" and "A frame" is discrimination training.

Discriminative Stimulus

Abbreviated S^D — a stimulus which signals that a particular response will be reinforced. Cues are discriminative stimuli. There is a trend to refer to the discriminative stimulus as the Evocative Stimulus which is abbreviated S^{EV}

Displacement Behaviors

Also called signs of stress, or distance increasing signals. Any behavior exhibited by a pet that is associated with anxiety or stress. Individual ethograms can be very helpful in identifying displacement behaviors. Sniffing and scratching are common displacement behaviors.

Dissonance

Cognitive dissonance is the condition of having inconsistent beliefs, thoughts and behaviors. Humans are motivated to minimize or eliminate facts which counter their current beliefs by adding new cognitions or by changing cognitions or by engaging in behavioral patterns that favor consonance. Ex. I love my pet. I use a shock collar on my pet. Shock collars cause pain and fear. My thoughts and actions are inconsistent. I can resolve this inconsistency by changing my actions. I stop using the shock collar.

Distractors

Proofs - Objects, people or other pets placed in a fashion to present the pet with options that are 'distractions' from the ideal choice. Distraction training ideally maintains a 90% success rate in order to pattern success rather than failure. Distractors may also be naturally occurring environmental stimuli.

DogSmith Poker

The train-test train method to ensure that when teaching a pet a new skill, the behavior is built at the correct criteria and there is an adequate amount or reinforcement taking place. Each set of behaviors at the current criteria is performed in 5 individual trials. If the behavior is successfully achieved 4 or 5 times out of 5 then the criteria in the next set can be increased in either duration, intensity or distance or a reduced latency. If the set of behaviors at the current criteria is only achieved 3 times then the trainer has the option to stick, repeat the set again, drop the criteria or change the setting events making the behavior more likely. Less than 3 correct responses should result in a drop of criteria to ensure the pet is successful and the rate of reinforcement is increased.

Domestication

A change in the phenotypical expression and genotype of a pet, population of animals or plants, through a process of selection, in order to make traits that benefit humans more prominent.

Dominance

A theory that is used with social pets within the same species to predict the winner of a conflict when fighting over a specific, context-oriented resource. Scientifically, dominance only applies to two beings of the same species, thus a human cannot be dominant over a pet nor can a pet be dominant over a human. In a wolf pack the dominant beings are the wolf pups; however, wolf researchers have moved away from alpha terminology and are now using terms that correspond with the role of the particular pet in the family unit.

Dopamine

A neurotransmitter known to affect motivation, movement and emotional responses.

Drive

Common term. The "energy" that activates a pet to attempt to meet a real or perceived need. This term is often used interchangeably with motivation. Ex. The pet is high drive - he demands work by pacing and having difficulty relaxing if he has not been exercised for an hour a day.

Duration Behavior

A behavior that must persist for a specific period of time. Ex. A down stay that lasts for two minutes.

E

Elicit

A term that applies to Respondent Conditioning and reflexive behaviors. These behaviors are not under voluntary control and thus are elicited by the pet in contrast to evoked which is a behavior that is under voluntary control and subject to Operant Conditioning. Eye blinks, emotions and digestive juices are all examples of elicited behaviors.

Emotion

A coordinated state that adjusts to behavioral and physiological responses to stimuli in order to motivate behavior to take advantage of opportunities or to cope with stress.

Emotional Contagion

The phenomenon by which an emotional state spreads from one being to another. Ex. One pet starts to show fear of a trash can, so the second pet also becomes fearful. Pet owner tenses and holds her breath and her pet starts barking and lunging at an unfamiliar pet. A pet owner becomes animated or excited and the pet responds in a similar way.

Empathy

The ability to identify and "feel" the emotion of another being. Higher empathy is associated with being more effective at identifying another being's modes of thought and moods. Empathy has been proven to exist in many mammals including: mice, rats and pets.

Epigenesis

The interaction of a beings' genes and environment in determining the expression of traits, via gene activation or deactivation, during development. Epigenetic processes are the result of intense long-term learning.

Ethology

The study of the biology of behavior by understanding causes and consequences of behavior developmentally and physiologically.

Ethogram

Comprehensive gathering and catalogue of behavioral signals showing relationships between beings of a species.

Errorless Learning

An ideal way of training making use of training approximations that do not include failures of any single trial.

Escape

Any training procedure that relies on the pet desiring to flee or move away from aversive stimulation. Escape is the means by which negative reinforcement functions. For example, you can't escape the annoying "ding, ding, ding" in your car unless you fasten your seat belt.

Establishing Operations (EO)

A change that can increase the effectiveness or value of a certain reinforcer.

Ex. If you have your pet skip a meal prior to a training session you are establishing operations so that your pet will be hungry and be motivated to work for food.

See Motivating Operations.

Evocative Stimulus

See Discriminative Stimulus

Evoke

A term that applies to Operant Conditioning and voluntary behaviors. In psychology the term is 'emitted'. These behaviors are said to be under voluntary control, so the pet can choose to perform them, in contrast to elicited behaviors which are reflexive and not under voluntary control. Sit, downs, obedience or agility behaviors are all evoked behaviors.

Exploratory Behavior

Investigative behavior that helps a pet gather information about an unfamiliar or novel environment, related to curiosity. Exploratory behavior functions to minimize stress associated with novelty.

Extinction or Extinguishing

A procedure which can occur Operantly and/or Respondently. When the reinforcement for the behavior is withheld or removed then this leads to a gradual cessation of behavior. See Respondent Extinction and Operant Extinction for more details.

Extinction Burst

A sudden, but usually temporary, increase in a behavior that occurs when withholding the consequence for a previously reinforced behavior. The previously reinforced behavior may also become more variable in an attempt to elicit reinforcement.

Evolution

Evolution, the change in traits of a population over a period of time is influenced by natural selection and adaptive behaviors. If a species cannot learn and adapt within its environment, then it would not survive.

Fading

Fading is how stimulus control is transferred from the prompt, verbal prompt, environmental prompt or physical prompt, to the final stimulus. The existing prompt, stimulus that exerts control over the behavior, is gradually faded away as the stimulus control is passed to the new stimulus. The old stimulus is faded away while the behavior has a high probability of reinforcement to avoid S^Δ, the extinction stimulus, and to eliminate errors. This is called errorless learning. During the fading procedure stimulus control is transferred by decreasing the level of prompts and by delaying the timing for presenting prompts.

Failure to Generalize

A lack of generalization refers to a scenario where the pet is not able to perform the trained behavior in a variety of settings. Once a behavior is under stimulus control, trainers should endeavor to practise the behavior in different locations, with appropriate (gradually increasing) levels of distractors.

Feedback

Feedback is input from another party on the action, process or results you are achieving.

Fixed Action Pattern

See Modal Action Pattern

Fixed Interval Schedule

A schedule of reinforcement that dictates that the first correct response after a set amount of time has passed is reinforced (i.e., a consequence is delivered). The time period required is always the same, therefore predictable to the pet.

Fixed Ratio Schedule

A schedule of reinforcement that is intermittent which makes use of a contingency such as the pet emitting a certain number of responses prior to being reinforced. Ex. The pet touches his nose to the palm of your hand five times before you click and treat. This is a fixed ratio schedule of reinforcement FR 5:1.

Flooding

Flooding is used in exposure therapy. The term refers to exposing the pet to a stimulus they are actively avoiding or seeking to escape. Flooding should always be avoided as it can lead to fear, anxiety, stress and learned helplessness. Systematic Desensitization is the preferred method for altering a pet's response to a stimulus.

Fluency

The goal of training, a combination of accuracy and fast response to a cue. The pet can effortlessly carry out the behavior. Ex. The trainer, while doing a jumping jack, says "sit" and the pet immediately sits.

Force

Force is a difficult term to define. Any definition can never be so expansive and explicit that every possible situation is addressed. This is seen everywhere in life and most obviously in the US legal system where very often courts cannot agree on a single interpretation of what terms and definitions mean, including physical force.

Recognizing this we understand, in the context of our dictionary and as a general framework, physical force to mean "any intentional physical act against a pet that causes psychological or physical pain, harm or damage to the pet."

Force Free Training

Training that minimizes stress for the pet. Force -Free Training by the definition of the Pet Professional Guild is No shock, No pain, No choke, No fear, No physical force, No compulsion based methods are ever employed to train or care for a pet.

Forward Chaining

In contrast to back chaining in forward(s) chaining the first component of the behavior chain is trained, followed by the first and second, followed by each subsequent behavior. Chaining is an appropriate procedure to employ when training two or more component behaviors that will be performed in sequence, with one cue used to evoke the final compound behavior.

Forward Conditioning

See conditioning.

Functional Assessment

The Functional Assessment is the behavior analytical approach to explaining, describing and controlling behavior. The behavior analytical approach does not rely on guess work, trial and error tactics or anecdotal recommendations but systematically identifies the functional relationship the behavior has with the environment. When these relationships have been identified then efficient and effective solutions can be developed. The intended final product of the Functional Assessment is a contingency statement that the behaviorist has confidence in. The contingency statement details in simple terms the antecedents, behaviors and consequences in measurable terms.

Function of the Behavior

Any variable maintaining a behavior is the function of the behavior. These things are: reinforcers, attention seeking, avoidance, escape and sensory reinforcers. Ex. A Border Collie requires no food or toy reinforcement for staring at the pet chasing the disc because watching movement is the function of the watching behavior.

Functional Analysis

The functional analysis is a third method and often the last method of choice for functionally assessing behavior. This is where we test the relationship between the behavior and its environment; we conduct an experimental study.

The functional analysis is a single subject experiment that tests the consultant's hypothesis, the contingency statement. The functional analysis should only be carried out if the initial interview and direct observation did not reveal trends in the problem behavior and or components of the contingency statement are still unclear. A functional analysis should be performed by a trained professional with a minimally invasive approach, a clearly defined plan to test only what is necessary and with careful consideration to the safety and security of all involved. There must also be consent from the pet's guardian and the pet's behavior must be measured, pre, during and post any intervention.

The functional analysis is designed to test the relationship between the hypothesized controlling antecedents and the behavior and/or the hypothesized maintaining relationship between the behavior and its consequence.

The functional analysis sets up different independent variables and confirms or refutes their effect on the dependent variable. The goal is to analysis what is and what is not evoking and or maintaining the behavior so that an effective behavior change program can be designed. The experiment should only cover areas of the contingency statement that are unclear and not everything. The consultant must also take into consideration, during the experiment, that setting events and motivating operations should not be overlooked as they can contribute indirectly to the contingencies.

Determining the Antecedent and Consequence of a specific behavior which a specific individual is emitting. Ex. A pet is barking at a garbage truck: Antecedent is the arrival of the garbage truck; the behavior is the barking, and the consequence is that the truck moves away! Antecedent Control protocols can be a great way to modify the problem of barking at garbage trucks. A way to double check your work of functionally analyzing a behavior is to be sure that you have an environment, followed by behavior, followed by environment.

Free Shaping or Free Behavior Shaping

Free refers to the lack of guidance from the trainer in the process of shaping by approximation. The ultimate example of free shaping is using a Skinner box in which only the being is present.   Free shaping requires a high level of skill from the trainer to avoid unnecessary frustration in the pet. Guided shaping, also called Micro Shaping, is generally a better choice for training, especially if accuracy is valued. Guided shaping makes use of a training plan in which the final goal behavior has been broken down into appropriate criteria and may include visual prompts; targeting; luring after the click, via placement of the reinforcer, and physical barriers to decrease random sampling.

G

Generalization

A scenario where the pet is able to perform the trained operant behavior in a variety of settings. Once a behavior is under stimulus control, trainers should endeavor to practise the behavior in different locations, with appropriate, gradually increasing, levels of 'distractors' (competing environmental stimuli). With respondent conditioning the conditioned response generalizes from the conditioned stimuli to other stimuli.

Generalized Settings

Any environment outside of the original one where the behavior in question was taught. Ex. If you taught your pet to sit in the kitchen, then any other room in the house or any area outside of the house is a Generalized Setting.

Generalized Conditioned Reinforcer

A reinforcer that is supported by many other reinforcers. In human terms, money is an example of a GCR as it can be used to access lots of things

Genotype

The actual genetic make up of the pet

Habituate or Habituation

A decreased response to a stimulus after prolonged exposure to a stimulus. Ex. You move into a house next to a railway line and initially cannot sleep because of the noise of the trains. After a couple of weeks, you no longer hear the trains

Hierarchy

A system in which individuals are ranked according to their level of authority or status, often depicted as a pyramid or ladder.

Hierarchy of Reinforcers

Common term: Hierarchy of Rewards.

A classification of an individual dog's positive reinforcement consequences from 'lower value' (least desirable) to highest value (most desirable). Before beginning any training, the trainer should make sure that the pet's basic needs are met. The trainer can then make use of both primary and secondary reinforcers but must bear in mind that the 'value' will be ascertained by the recipient and not the provider.

Hierarchy of Needs

When needs are not being met, pets will be motivated to try and fulfil those needs. Psychologist Abraham Maslow's Hierarchy of Needs is a motivational theory in psychology, often depicted as hierarchical levels within a pyramid. Maslow stated that people are motivated to achieve certain needs and that some needs take precedence over others. The Hierarchy of Needs includes: Biological and physiological needs; Safety needs; Love and belongingness needs; Esteem needs; Cognitive needs; Aesthetic needs; Self-actualization needs; Transcendence needs.

Hierarchy of Dogs Needs

The Hierarchy of Dog Needs, adapted by Pet Professional Guild Member Linda Michaels from Maslow's Hierarchy of Needs, is a hierarchical model of wellness and behavior modification in which first we meet our dogs' biological, emotional and social needs and, once these foundational needs have been met, we use management, antecedent modification, positive and differential reinforcement, counter-conditioning and desensitization to modify behavior.

High Order Conditioning

High order conditioning takes place when a well-established conditioned stimulus is paired with a neutral stimulus to elicit a conditioned response. High order conditioning takes place in the absence of an unconditioned stimulus. With high order conditioning many more stimuli can come to elicit conditional responses not just those paired with an unconditioned stimulus, thus enhancing the ability of the pet to adapt and survive. High order conditioning also affects and influences many emotional reactions such as fear.

Imprinting

The capacity to learn certain types of information at specific critical learning periods associated with development. Critical learning periods are also called sensitive periods or fear periods.

Imitation

Social Learning. In behavior analysis this word is reserved for actions or sounds that are copied. The teacher models the behavior and the student imitates. The DogNostics Copy Cat Protocol, Do as I Do (Claudia Fugazza & Ken Ramirez) and Copy That (Pat Miller) are all examples of teaching by imitation. Ex. In pushball humans can get on all fours and push the ball with their nose below the mid-section of the ball. The pet copies the action and pushes the ball.

Impulsiveness

Impulsivity. Acting without thinking about the consequence. A lack of self-control commonly seen in young dogs and those lacking polite manners.

Impulse Control

Pets that lack impulse control struggle to resist the urge to act, usually have decreased bite inhibition and take longer to learn duration behaviors. Lack of impulse control usually responds well to self-control training games; teaching the dog good manners and calm behaviors.

Informant Interview

The informant interview is the first component of a Functional Assessment where anecdotal information is gathered from the pet owners. This information is gathered through in-person interviews, questionaries' and email correspondence.

Inter-Trial Interval

The time between one trial and the next trial. When working in sets of five trials the ITL is the time between each of the five trials.

Instrumental Learning

Another term for Operant Conditioning.

Intermittent Reinforcement

Reinforcement that is not continuous. Intermittent reinforcement is more resistant to extinction than continuous reinforcement. Intermittent Interval Schedules are based on the passage of time. Intermittent Ratio Schedules are based on the number of responses.

Intermittent Bridging

The technique of intermittently reinforcing after the bridging stimulus, often used in zoos or in marine animal training, where the trainer clicks the correct response but does not deliver a primary reinforcer. Not recommended.

Intrinsic vs. Extrinsic Reinforcement

Intrinsic reinforcement is considered a reinforcement that the pet gets from engaging in an activity rather than, extrinsic reinforcement where the pet receives a tangible reinforcer from the trainer.

Involuntary Behavior

Respondent conditioning deals with involuntary behaviors. These are reflexive behaviors that are not consciously controlled.

J

Jackpot

A term used to describe a special type of reinforcement where more food, additional play or more quantity or quality of reinforcer is being used.

Jolly Routine

A training tool that makes use of emotional contagion by the owner and/or trainer behaving cheerfully to prompt a happy emotional state in the pet being trained. Often used in situations that are potentially scary to the pet to avoid fear and stress and to encourage resilience.

Jump Start

Also called a sampling of the reinforcer. When a trainer allows the pet to smell, see or sniff the appetitive reinforcer to help create motivation in the pet.

K

Keep Going Signal

Continuation Bridge: An auditory or visual signal that indicates to the pet that it is carrying out the correct response and should continue; reinforcement will be delivered at the end of the behavior or chain. Ex. In the 1960s Bob Bailey developed a "Keep Going System" for the military in which cats, that had microphones implanted in them, were directed to keep going in a specific direction via the continuation of a specific sound.

Keep Going Signals are most effective when previously conditioned as secondary reinforcers.

L

Latency

The time period between the cue and the initiation of the behavior. Fluency is attained if you have minimal latency. Ex. Trainer says "sit" – pet sits immediately within less than one second.

Latent Learning

A form of learning that occurs without any obvious reinforcement and is not behaviorally observable until a later time. Latent learning demonstrates that reinforcement does not need to be present for learning to occur.

Learned Helplessness

In the phenomenon called learned helplessness, a pet is first exposed to inescapable and severe aversive stimulation. Eventually the pet gives up and stops attempting to avoid or escape the situation. Common term: Shut down. Inexperienced trainers may label the pet as 'calm'.

Learned Irrelevance

Also called the pre-exposure effect. A psychological phenomenon that occurs when repeated exposure to a stimulus not connected to a contingency causes the stimulus to become meaningless. There is no fear present when learned irrelevance occurs, instead it addresses how repeated cues or other stimuli can come to become meaningless.

Learned Laziness

A problematic contingency when a pet has been exposed to non-contingent reinforcement for a period of time resulting in a pet that is lacking motivation. This is most often seen in pets that are on a free feeding schedule and are given treats non-contingently on a consistent basis.

Learning

A measurable change in behavior as a result of an experience. Learning does not impact how an individual behaves; it impacts the individual's ability to modify its behavior given a different set of events.

Learning Set

The phenomenon that occurs when a pet learns the patterns by which he is being trained and thus is able to learn more quickly. This is why force free training is such a great gift to pet trainers: It helps pets learn to learn, increasing their abilities to problem solve. This ability can then be applied to other learning situations.

Least Reinforcing Stimulus

Developed by marine animal trainers, a form of negative punishment where the trainer goes to a neutral response. This is referred to as the LRS. To avoid fall out and counter control from frustration, the LRS is put on a very infrequent variable reinforcement schedule. Also called No Change Response. Ex. Trainer gives the cue: "down", pet sits instead, trainer goes neutral for five seconds.

Limited Hold or Limited Hold Schedule

The first response after a specific period of time is reinforced. For the purpose of pet training, Limited Holds are used to reduce latency and increase frequency. Ex. Trainer says "sit." If the pet immediately sits, the trainer clicks and treats. If the pet does not sit quickly there is no click and treat. Only fast responses to the cue "sit" are reinforced.

Limbic System

The area and pathways in the mammalian brain that controls emotional behaviors, feelings and moods.

Loading

As in "loading the clicker" — the respondent process of creating an association between the clicker sound, a neutral stimulus and the unconditioned stimulus, food. This pairing results in the clicking sound taking on reinforcing properties. By pairing the click with a treat, the click itself becomes reinforcing to the pet. This loading process is not permanent; it is possible to click repeatedly and not reinforce and eventually the "loading" will regress, the association is no longer there as the clicker has lost its predictive value.

L-Theanine

An amino acid nutritional supplement often used with pets that has prompted improvement for many pets that have problematic emotional responses such as fear. Vets sell the supplements as Composure and Anxitane both of which have been shown to reduce fear and anxiety in pets. There are no known levels of toxicity of L-Theanine in humans or rodents.

Lumping and Splitting

Accidentally or deliberately combining training criteria to the point where it is confusing to the pet is lumping. Splitting, or slicing, breaks down behaviors or behavior chains to an ideal training plan with appropriate criteria.

Luring or Prompting

Prompts are antecedents as they come before the behavior, they can be food, targets, verbal prompts. Lures and prompts, while able to get behavior quickly, require the additional work of fading them out of the final behavior topography.

M

Magnitude

An emitted behavior's level of magnitude is based on the intensity of the behavior. The loudness of a bark or the force of motor responses. Ex. A terrier trained to close the door on the cue of "close" leaps at the door with such magnitude that the door loudly slams shut.

Maintenance

The phase of training in which stimulus control has been attained. Cue response occurs both accurately and with minimal latency. The proofing part of the training process has been completed. Ex. The pet sits on cue even when the trainer lies on the floor or calls the cue from another room.

Management

Preventing the pet from being exposed to the antecedent stimulus. An important tool in behavior modification as it prevents the rehearsal of the undesired behavior. Ex. Pet's trainer moves the pet behind a car to prevent the pet from seeing the stranger. The pet therefore does not rehearse barking and lunging.

Marker

Also called bridging stimulus. A word, sound or stimulus that is a secondary reinforcer used to 'mark' the correct behavioral response – "Yes, that is right". The marker acts as a bridge – a connection between the behavior and the reinforcer – and a cue which signals a positive reinforcement consequence is coming. Ex. The click sound of the clicker.

Matching Law

Matching law suggests that when different schedules of reinforcement are available at the same time for different behaviors the pet will behave according to the relative rates of reinforcement available for each behavior performed.

Therefore, the pet will engage, exhibit more of the behavior that produces the highest levels of reinforcement and thus less of the behavior that produces less reinforcement.

Mean

The mean is another way of saying average in numerical terms.

Medical Model

The medical model perspective on behavior is that behaviors can be categorized, labeled and treated with standardized protocols. Unlike the ethological, psychological and medical mode orientation the behavioral perspective on behavior is that behavior is a function of its environment and that environmental stimuli cause behavior as opposed to genetics.

Memory

A key component of learning is the ability to recall a previous event and its circumstances. A pet cannot learn contingencies or associations without memory. Ex. Pet remembers that the last five times he sat at the door while greeting a stranger he got clicks and treats, so he sits at the door when the doorbell rings.

Measurement

The act of measuring a unit by size, weight, frequency, dimension, latency. In applied behavior analysis we must first measure baseline behaviors and then process data to ensure our intervention practices are having the desired goal impact on the behavior. Post measurement systems are put into place upon reaching the goal to ensure the maintenance protocols required are working too.

Micro-Shaping

A term coined by Kay Laurence. Behaviors are shaped with a 95-100% reinforcement rate, slicing the behaviors very finely to build only the desired actions. There is a clear base position. The learning is self-directed, and the learner is given limited choice through setting up the environment in such a way as to promote the correct response. Various reinforcement patterns are used. Puzzle moments are introduced to test the behavior/what the dog has learned. Micro shaping involves a process of micro-extinction, not macro.

Merged Behavior

A behavior that is comprised of different behaviors which are then combined into a final result. Not to be confused with a behavior chain which is a sequence of behaviors. Ex. A retrieve over a jump (The pet collects a dumbbell and jumps while holding the dumbbell in his mouth.)

Mirror Neurons

Neurons which fire when a pet is performing a specific behavior or watching another pet perform a behavior.

Modal Action Pattern

Formerly referred to as Fixed Action Pattern. MAP's are instinctive or innate behaviors. An innate pattern of coordinated behaviors that have a somewhat fixed form and need not to be learned.

Modeling

See Imitation.

Molding

Environmental Molding: The trainer makes use of the environment, including props and barriers, to help facilitate the teaching process by limiting the choices available to the pet and guiding towards the desired behavioral response.

Molding by Contact: A light touch is employed to suggest the desired behavioral response. For example, the trainer would like the pet to lift the front left paw and so lightly touches that paw, communicating with the pet which paw to lift. Please note, this is not the manipulation of a pet into position. Molding should not involve pressure.

Motivating Operations

Motivating operations affect and influence the value of the reinforcer and therefore increase or decrease the likelihood of the discriminative stimulus to evoke the behavior . Emotional Responses can also be considered Motivating Operations as they impact the value of the reinforcement.

Motivation

Motivation can be described as the direction and persistence of action. Common characteristics of motivation are that motivation is typified as an individual phenomenon, motivation is described usually as intentional and motivation is multifaceted. The purpose of motivational theories is to predict behavior.

Multiple Contingencies

Term that describes a learning situation where multiple layers of learning are taking place. Ex. Owner sprays pet with vinegar water when he barks. Pet learns to stop barking. Pet learns spray bottles are scary. Pet learns to move away quickly when his owner raises his arm.   The intent of the owner was to address the barking but because of multiple contingencies more problematic learning was also taking place.

Natural Selection

Darwin proposed that species adapt to changes in their environment. The individual features that directly contribute to a species survival, such as innate behaviors, reflexes, modal action patterns and general behavior traits are said to be selected by the environment, This Darwin termed natural selection.

Negative Contrast

A decrease of motivation as a result of the presentation of a lower value reinforcer after the presentation of a high value reinforcer. Ex. The trainer runs out of liverwurst, so she switches to kibble. The pet is barely motivated by the kibble, loses focus and eventually quits working.

Negative Punishment

A procedure that involves the pet losing access to something they desire. Ex. Taking away the food bowl, removing the cookie from the pet's nose, or withdrawing your attention are all examples of negative punishment. Another example is timing your pet out in another room for twenty seconds to two minutes. Longer periods of time out are not advisable as the pet may get bored and is less likely to create an association between cause and effect.

Negative Reinforcement

The continuation of an aversive stimulus until the compliance of the pet is obtained at which point the aversive stimulus is removed. This procedure that can range from mildly to severely aversive to the pet. Repeatedly yanking on your pet's leash to force her into heel position is an example of negative reinforcement.

Neuroplasticity

The ability of neurons to change over a long period of time with intense exposure to learning. Can be modest after learning or remarkable after trauma.

Neurotransmitter

A biochemical that is released at one end of a nerve cell which then acts on the receptor of the next nerve cell.

Neutral Stimulus

An antecedent stimulus, in Respondent Conditioning, that has no effect on the behavior that is elicited.

No Change Response

See least reinforcing stimulus.

Non-Affective Aggression

See predation

Non-Associative Learning

A change in reflexive behavior that is the result of exposure to stimuli that are not associated with behavior consequences. Habituation and sensitization are non-associative learning.

Non-Contingent Reinforcement

Giving a pet access to plentiful amounts of reinforcement to prevent them from engaging in a problematic behavior

Non-Violent Communication

A process of communicating that enables constructive positive dialogue. The process follows a three-step process: 1. Empathize 2. Identify feelings 3. Address needs.

Novel Stimuli

An occurrence that the pet has not previously experienced. Ex. A four-week-old puppy walks on grass for the first time. Grass is the novel stimulus.

O

One Trial Learning

A single presentation of behavior consequence resulting in changes in behavior.

Operant Aggression

Aggression that is reinforced by the removal of an aversive stimulus via Negative Reinforcement

Operant Conditioning

There are four types of operant learning, defined as such because the behavior operates on the environment. Two of the quadrants of operant conditioning strengthen behaviors, referred to as reinforcements. The other two of the operant conditioning quadrants weaken behavior, referred to as punishments. The quadrants are referred to as a negative reinforcement, positive reinforcement, negative punishment and positive punishment. The terms positive and negative do not describe the consequence, they indicate whether a stimulus, has been added (positive) or subtracted (negative) to increase or weaken the preceding behavior.

Both positive and negative reinforcement increase the strength of the behavior due to its consequence.

With positive reinforcement the behavior is followed by the appearance of or an increase in the intensity of a stimulus. The stimulus is called a positive reinforcement as it is something the subject seeks out therefore it reinforces the behavior that precedes it.

With negative reinforcement the behavior is strengthened by the subject's ability to avoid or escape an aversive stimulus, thus negative reinforcement is sometimes referred to as escape-avoidance learning. An experience must have three characteristics to qualify as reinforcement. The behavior must have a consequence, the behavior must increase in strength and the increase in strength must be a result of the consequence.

As behavior is the function of its consequences and whereas reinforcement strengthens the likelihood of a behavior then punishments reduce the strength of the behavior. Punishers are aversives and something a subject works to avoid. When an aversive event is added to a situation then positive punishment has taken place. Negative punishment subtracts something from the situation, like privileges, and is sometimes called penalty training. Experiences must have three characteristics to qualify as punishment. First, the behavior must have a consequence, second the behavior must decrease in strength and finally the reduction in strength must be a result of the consequence.

Operant Class

A group of behaviors that share a similar consequence but may vary in their topography.

Operant Extinction

Operant extinction is when the consequences that reinforced a behavior are withheld and the strength of the behavior is weakened. The goal of operant extinction is to reduce the frequency of the behavior. Operant extinction can also increase the frequency of emotional behaviors such as aggression. See extinction burst.

Opposition Reflex

Common Term used to describe a dog's resistance to coercion often quoted with reference to the handler pulling one way and the dog resisting or pulling in the opposite direction. Sometimes called the balancing reflex. The opposition reflex is when a pet leans into pressure rather than yielding to it (scientifically known as positive thigmotaxis). An unhelpful label. Trainers should observe and define the behavior and understand the cause and consequence.

Optimal Foraging Theory

The behavioral economics of nature. Pets will forage expending the least amount of energy for the most amount of food.

Overshadowing

In respondent conditioning, if two or more conditioned stimuli occur at the same time, only the most strongly perceived or salient stimulus will be processed. Overshadowing is related to stimulus salience as the strongest stimulus is the most salient one. The salient stimulus will overshadow the weaker stimulus.

Ex. Present a verbal "yes", and a click at the same time, and then feed to create a conditioning effect. After conditioning takes place, pet is drooling. Test both separately and find that only the click elicits the conditioned response. The more salient, more noticeable, click was conditioned and the verbal "yes" was overshadowed.

Pack Theory

A theory based on wolf research that states that pets form linear hierarchies led by alphas. This term has been inaccurately used to describe canine groups and label specific behaviors. Pack theory in wolves and the term 'alpha' has largely been replaced by the terms family unit and breeders or breeding pair.

Pair or Pairing

The process by which associative learning, also known as respondent conditioning, takes place. One stimulus is associated with another and reliably predicts the other stimulus. Ex. The click is paired with the treat.

Parallel Play

When two pets engage in similar play, not with each other but simultaneously.

Pattern Training

Also called patterning or overlearning. Doing a large number of repetitions in the high hundreds to low thousand, in an attempt to "program" a pet into responding a specific way.

Performance

The behavior that is actually observed is the pet's performance.

Pet Cognition

The study of memory, attention, learning, reasoning, problem solving and signal and verbal communication in pets.

Ping-Ponging

This term was first referenced in print by Morgan Spector in "Clicker Training for Obedience." Ping-ponging refers to bouncing your criteria gently back and forth while still slowly increasing it.

Play

An expression of motor patterns that appears self-reinforcing. Play creates emotional states incompatible with fear, anxiety and stress. Categories of play are: object, locomotor, and social play.

Poisoned Cue

A cue trained with negative reinforcement will become a negative discriminative stimulus. A cue trained with positive reinforcement will become a positive discriminative stimulus. Therefore, a cue trained with unpleasant consequences is "poisoned" because it does not take on reinforcing properties.

Post-Reinforcement Pause

A pause in responding following reinforcement; associated with fixed interval or fixed ratio schedules of reinforcement (Paul Chance). If your pattern of reinforcing becomes predictable to the pet, you may get a post-reinforcement pause - the pet temporarily shows a decrease in motivation until she anticipates the time of potential reinforcement is closer.

Post Traumatic Growth

A positive psychology term, referring to the process by which a traumatic incident becomes the opportunity for new learning and growth resulting in a better emotional outcome than prior to the traumatic incident. Ex. A pet is jumped by a stray pet and is physically and mentally injured. Prior to the incident this pet did not like pets, after the incident the pet is consistently barking and lunging at other pets.

Positive Contrast

The opposite of negative contrast. This term refers to the pet's rate of response increasing as a result of delivery of reinforcement that is of higher value than the norm (also known as the elation effect) Ex. The agility pet began running agility faster when the trainer started to use freeze dried lobster treats.

Positive Punishment

As behavior is the function of its consequences and whereas reinforcement strengthens the likelihood of a behavior then punishments reduce the strength of the behavior. Punishers are aversives and something a subject works to avoid. When an aversive event is added to a situation then positive punishment has taken place. See operant conditioning also

Positive Reinforcement

With positive reinforcement the behavior is followed by the appearance of or an increase in the intensity of a stimulus. The stimulus is called a positive reinforcement as it is something the subject seeks out therefore it reinforces the behavior that precedes it. See operant conditioning.

Positive Training

A training philosophy where the trainer utilizes positive operant and respondent conditioning protocols as their go-to choice.

Predatory Drift

A pet trainer term that refers to the modal action patterns related to predation. The phenomena that can occur when dogs suddenly go into predation mode. This can be evoked by certain sounds or movements that trigger a predatory response in a dog. This predatory behavior functions as a general behavior trait. Predatory drift can sometimes occur when dog play suddenly turns into conflict. A fast-moving small dog who makes high pitched sounds can trigger predatory drift from a larger dog.

Predation

Non-affective, predatory aggression uses the predatory sequence. These are general behavior traits in our pet dogs. Non-affective, predatory aggression does not provoke the sympathetic nervous system, the emotional system and it is very different to affective aggression. Dogs do not bite because they are emotionally aroused, they bite because of a predatory action pattern.

Preference

When there are several reinforcement opportunities for a pet the one they choose to engage in is their preference

Preference Test

A test conducted by a trainer to help determine what a pet's preference is when there are multiple competing contingencies

Premack Principle or Reinforcer

The Relativity Theory of Reinforcement. Using access to a desired activity as a means of positively reinforcing a less desired activity. Ex. A Border Collie prefers playing disc, over heeling, so trainer asks pet to heel before playing disc. As a result, heeling predicts play with the disc and heeling becomes more fun to the Border Collie. Common Term: Grandma's Rule.

Primacy

This effect shows that when memorizing a sequence, things that occur early in the chain or things that occur later in the chain are more easily memorized. It suggests why phone numbers are interrupted with gaps or dashes which creates more beginnings and endings, making them easier to memorize. It argues that for example, ending a training session with a "jackpot" may influence memory *not* because of the "jackpot" but rather because of the recency effect.

Primary Reinforcer

A reinforcer that does not require any learning to be reinforcing: food and water are examples. There is much debate amongst trainers as to whether tactile reinforcement (physical touch) can be considered a primary reinforcement.

Proactive Training

Training that makes use of antecedent control, management and the generating and increasing of reinforcement history rather than manipulating postcedents, consequences. Any training that focuses on the pre-behavior area of the three-term contingency.

Prompts/Prompting

Prompts in training are antecedents that help a behavior occur. They are not always part of the end behavior and therefore need to be faded out as the behavior is acquired.

Prompt Dependency

When the pet cannot perform the cued behavior without the prompt being present   This is why it is recommended that prompts be rapidly faded. Ex. The terrier would not perform any manners on cue unless food was in the trainer's hand. The terrier's manners are prompt dependent.

Projection

A psychological mechanism that causes one person to assign their own short-comings to another.

Proofing

The four key stages of learning are Acquisition, Fluency, Generalization and Maintenance. Proofing is part of the generalization stage of learning, in which the pet is taught to respond to a discriminative stimulus in the presence of varying environmental stimuli. Distance, Duration and Distractions, often referred to as the 3 Ds, are an essential component to proofing a behavior. Behaviors should be proofed before generalizing to different locations.

Punishment

 As behavior is the function of its consequences and whereas reinforcement strengthens the likelihood of a behavior then punishments reduce the strength of the behavior. Punishers are aversives and something a subject works to avoid. When an aversive event is added to a situation then positive punishment has taken place. Negative punishment subtracts something from the situation, like privileges, and is sometimes called penalty training. Experiences must have three characteristics to qualify as punishment. First, the behavior must have a consequence, second the behavior must decrease in strength and finally the reduction in strength must be a result of the consequence.

Punishment Fallout

Punishment creates many problems, particularly when the punishment is physical. Escape, aggression, apathy, abuse and imitation of the punisher are all fallouts of using punishment. Pets escape (try to avoid) the source of the punishment. Humans resort to "tuning out", lying and cheating as avoidance tactics. An alternative to escaping the source of the punishment is to attack the source. In some situations, the aggression is redirected at another pet or innate object. Punishment can create a conditioned emotional response to the stimuli that surrounds the punishment, strengthening escape, avoidance and aggressive behaviors.

Of the two types of punishment available negative punishment, removing a privilege as a consequence to an unwanted behavior, is less damaging than the application of physical, positive punishment. Punishment can work in the short term and therefore the application of punishment is reinforcing to the person administering the punishment. To be effective punishment has to be delivered immediately, be contingent on the behavior and delivered at the correct intensity with no conflicting reinforcement. These criteria are very difficult to meet and there is a high likelihood of errors in the application of the punishment. More often than not, the use of punishment does not meet the necessary criteria and does not eliminate behavior, it just suppresses it.

In the absence of aggression or escape (they are not available to the pet) the punishment can create apathetic behavior. The punishment not only suppresses the unwanted behavior but all behavior. Punishment tends to produce a global suppression of operant behavior. If the application of punishment itself is reinforcing to the person applying the punishment, then the punishing behavior will increase in strength or frequency. When punishment is applied at an introductory level and the consequences become stronger and stronger the end result can be abuse. Pets and people that are punished adopt punishment as a vehicle to deal with difficult situations perpetuating unwanted behavior.

Push, Drop, Stick

As taught by Jean Donaldson. Training in sets to recognize when criteria should be increased to the next level of difficulty, decreased to the previous level of difficulty or repeated at the same level. This ensures the pet remains motivated "in the game" as the levels of reinforcement are high and expectations for the individual pet realistic.

Q

Quadrants

There are four types of operant learning, defined as such because the behavior operates on the environment. Two of the quadrants of operant conditioning strengthen behaviors, referred to as reinforcements. The other two of the operant conditioning quadrants weaken behavior, referred to as punishments. The quadrants are referred to as a negative reinforcement, positive reinforcement, negative punishment and positive punishment. The terms positive and negative do not describe the consequence, they indicate whether a stimulus, has been added (positive) or subtracted (negative) to increase or weaken the preceding behavior

Rapid-Fire Clicking and Reinforcing

The act of repeatedly clicking and reinforcing in order to communicate to your pet that she is to hold the current position. This is often how a pet is taught to hold a sit, down, or stand position with the rate of reinforcement being gradually reduced as the reinforcement history is developed

Rate of Reinforcement

The number of reinforcers a pet is given in a specific time period. High rates of reinforcement mean a great deal of clicking and treating in a short period of time. Skilled shaping requires a high rate of reinforcement to avoid unnecessary frustration for the pet.

Ratio Strain

A sharp decrease in responding as a result of a reinforcement schedule being too quickly thinned out. Ex. A pet that is used to getting a click and a treat every time she performs a behavior is unable to perform five behaviors in a row without a treat.

Reflex

Reflexes are the relationship between a specific event and specific response. By nature, reflexes are stereotypic, but the strength of a reflex response can be altered through sensitization and habituation.

Redirection

When a trainer gently interrupts a pet and moves the pet's focus to another activity.

Reinforcement

Reinforcement increase the strength of the behavior due to its consequence.

Reinforcement History

All of the reinforcement contingencies a pet has been exposed to during its lifetime

Reinforcement Schedules

The time periods, duration or intervals required prior to the delivery of reinforcement.

Reinforcer Assessment

Evaluating what type of reinforcers and reinforcement an individual pet finds reinforcing. Usually some reinforcers are vastly preferred over others. This creates a hierarchy of reinforcers which is very valuable information to the trainer who can pair more highly valued reinforcers for more difficult behaviors.

Reinforcer Sampling

See Jump Start.

Relativity Theory of Reinforcement

See Premack Principle

Reset Cookie

A process that makes use of giving a free cookie or reinforcement that is non-contingent of the goal behavior to avoid loss of motivation. If you lose a pets' motivation you have nothing to train, thus the use of a reset cookie/treat, while undermining stimulus control, is valuable to the training process and likely falls within the realm of the art of training.

Resistance to Extinction

If a pet continues to perform the target behavior once reinforcement is taken away, is it called resistant to extinction. Behaviors reinforced variably are more resistant to extinction.

Respondent Conditioning

See Classical Conditioning

Respondent conditioning takes place when an unconditioned stimulus that elicits an unconditioned response is repeatedly paired with a neutral stimulus. As a result of conditioning, the neutral stimulus becomes a conditioned stimulus that reliably elicits a conditioned response. Each single pairing is considered a trial. With respondent conditioning the presentation of the two stimuli, neutral and unconditioned, are presented regardless of the behavior the individual is exhibiting. The behavior elicited is a reflex response.

Response Generalization

Part of generalization training. The pet changes the form of the target behavior but ends up with a behavior that serves the same function. In pet training this could be a pet that is taught a left finish by turning to his left, circling around and stopping in heel position. The response generalization occurs when this pet "invents" a flip finish which serves the same function but was not the behavior originally given.

Respondent Extinction

Respondent extinction is the process of repeatedly presenting a conditioned stimulus without presenting an unconditioned stimulus, so the conditioned response gets weaker and weaker. The conditioned stimulus – unconditioned stimulus contingency is dissolved

S

Salience

How noticeable or obvious a stimulus is. Discriminative Stimuli (cues) and Bridging Stimuli (behavior markers) need to be salient, standing out from other environmental stimuli. For example, a clicker is usually more salient than a verbal marker such as the word "yes".

Satiation

When repeated presentations of a reinforcer weaken the response then satiation has occurred. Ex: This can occur when a biological need has been met if you are reinforcing with food and the pet becomes full.

Scalloping

See Ratio Strain.

Schedules of Reinforcement

Continuous reinforcement is when behavior is reinforced each time it occurs, one reinforcer for one response schedule. Because each operant is reinforced the increase in the rate of behavior is rapid. However, with continuous reinforcement the pet responds until it is satiated. Continuous reinforcement offers little resistance to extinction and produces stereotyped response topography. Continuous reinforcement is rare in a natural environment where most behavior is reinforced on an intermittent schedule.

With intermittent schedules of reinforcement only some, not all, behavioral responses are reinforced. Intermittent schedules include ratio schedules of reinforcement and interval schedules of reinforcement.

Ratio schedules of reinforcement are based on a set number of responses given prior to reinforcement.

Interval schedules operate on a set amount of time having passed prior to reinforcement being delivered.

Both ratio and interval schedules can be on a fixed or a variable, random schedule of reinforcement.

Fixed ratio schedules produce a rapid run of responses followed by reinforcement and then a pause. The pause is referred to as the 'post reinforcement pause (PRP) and is influenced by the number of responses and the size of the reinforcer. It can be argued that continuous reinforcement is a fixed schedule (one response to one reinforcement - shown as FR: 1), where each behavior response is reinforced. If fixed ratio schedules are carefully engineered a gradual increase in the ratio requirements can support more behavior for a single delivery of reinforcement.

Variable ratio schedules for reinforcement are based around an average of fixed ratios of different sizes Variable ratio schedules produce a faster response in behavior than fixed rate schedules as the 'pause after reinforcement' is reduced if not eliminated when the ratio contingency is changed from fixed to variable.

Interval type intermittent schedules provide reinforcement after a period of time not after a set number of responses.

Like ratio schedules, interval schedules can be on a fixed or variable sequence.   Unlike fixed ratio schedules that reinforce steady performance and yield a steady run rate, fixed interval schedules provide a characteristic pattern of response called scalloping. After reinforcement there is a pause, followed by a few probing responses followed by rapid responses as the interval times out. Scalloping occurs because pets produce more responses than the interval schedule requires because they cannot tell the time.

Variable interval schedules provide reinforcement after a variable period of time has passed. Variable interval schedules "produce high steady run rates, higher than fixed interval schedules". To increase the rate of response in a variable interval schedule you can set a rule that the reinforcement is only available for a set period of time. This rule is referred to as "limited hold" The "limited hold" rule can be used for all schedules of reinforcement. In general, ratio schedules produce a higher rate of behavior than interval schedules; they have shorter interresponse time - the time between any two responses.

Other schedules of reinforcement include duration schedules and time schedules. Duration schedules of reinforcement are contingent on a behavior being performed for a period of time. Fixed duration schedules require the behavior be performed for a set period of time whereas variable duration schedule works around some average. Each performance of behavior is reinforced after a different duration. Variable duration, like variable interval and variable ratio schedules, appear to be random but they are variable around a mean. With fixed duration and variable duration schedules, reinforcement may not be forthcoming. If the behavior itself does not provide intrinsic reinforcement the behavior may be weak.

Time schedules of reinforcement can also be fixed or variable. Time schedules of reinforcement deliver reinforcement independent of a behavior. These are referred to as noncontingent reinforcement schedules (NCR). Fixed time schedules are similar to fixed interval schedules except no behavior is required. Variable time schedules deliver reinforcement at irregular intervals regardless of the behavior.

Fixed time and variable time schedules deliver reinforcement with no regard to behavior but when no reinforcement is delivered this is considered extinction. Intermittent reinforcement schedules make extinction more difficult. When behavior is reinforced more regularly it has a lower momentum and is more readily extinguished (Pierce and Cheney 2004 p 126).

Secondary Reinforcer

Conditioned reinforcers, referred to as secondary reinforcers, are dependent on an association with other reinforcers. They owe their effectiveness directly or indirectly to primary reinforcers. Secondary, conditioned reinforcers tend to be weaker than primary, unconditioned reinforcers but they are more durable, more easily available and less disruptive than primary reinforcements. They are susceptible to extinction though if you don't follow them with unconditioned reinforcers.

Selectionism

Another term for shaping and differential reinforcement.

Self-Reinforcing

Any behavior that does not require external reinforcement in order to be maintained. The behavior itself is intrinsically reinforcing to the pet. The internal sensation of performing the behavior is reinforcing.

Sensitization or Sensitizing

Considered non-associative learning. Sensitization occurs when repeated exposure or a single exposure to a stimulus increases the intensity of the response. Thunderstorm phobia is an example of when a pet can become sensitized to a noise or visual stimulus.

Separation Anxiety or Distress

Evidence shows that separation distress related behaviors are respondent behaviors. They are a combination of the body's panic and fear systems. The amygdala, a section of the brain that stores memories associated with emotional events, activates behavioral and emotional responses to fear). Separation distress is defined as physical or behavioral signs of distress or in the absence of, or lack of access to a person, place or object.

Serotonin

A neurotransmitter found in the brain of mammals associated with learning, sleep, sensory perception, temperature regulation, and reducing anxiety.

Set

Repetition of five behaviors. Training in sets of five trials is a systematic method that helps trainers recognize whether to raise, lower or repeat the established criterion. See Push, Drop, Stick and DogSmith Poker

Setting Event

Setting events are general conditions that set the occasion for the behavior. Examples of setting events are medical problems, nutritional issues or lack of exercise. Setting events make the behavior in question more likely to occur. Setting events do not directly evoke the behavior but they provide a context in which the behavior is more likely to be evoked by the Stimulus.

Shaping

Reinforcing small approximations of a desired behavior in succession to achieve a more complicated behavior is called shaping. Behavior shaping can be used to achieve complicated behaviors that do not occur naturally or that are not in the pet's current repertoire. They cannot be captured or are too complicated to lure. See Micro-shaping.

Shaping Plan

Effective behavior shaping commences with a plan of the desired behavior and a detailed understanding of each behavior approximation to be reinforced. Shaping plans need to remain flexible. When shaping a behavior, you start by reinforcing small steps and giving immediate reinforcement. The reinforcers are small and easily delivered so the shaping is not delayed, and the pet does not get satiated too quickly. Once the pet can easily complete the first approximation of the behavior then the trainer moves onto the next approximation, they up the ante. This is done by putting the current criteria on extinction generates behavioral variability, from which you choose the next approximation.

Shared Meaning

The process of establishing norms in a behavior consultation or group class. Ex. Clearly defining what is expected of students and checking in and verifying that students have heard this information as intended.

Sign Stimulus

See Supernormal Stimulus.

Simultaneous Conditioning

One of the four ways conditioning takes place in Respondent Conditioning. With simultaneous conditioning the conditioned stimulus and unconditioned stimulus are presented at exactly the same time, as there is no interval between the conditioned stimulus and unconditioned stimulus it makes conditioning very ineffective. In respondent conditioning the amount of learning depends on the degree to which the conditioned stimulus predicts the unconditioned stimulus.

Single Event Learning

The process by which, during respondent conditioning or counterconditioning, one single exposure to an appetitive or aversive stimulus can result in an immediate conditioned response.

Skinnerian Conditioning

See Operant Conditioning.

Sleep

A state of rest and inactivity for mammals during which the pet is not responsive to external stimuli. Considering sleep duration and quality is an important part of a behavior consultation or any assessment.

Social Attraction

Social attraction refers to the level a pet consistently displays distance decreasing behaviors when in the presence of a person or people as a result of intrinsic and conditioned reinforcement. The same can apply to pets in which case the distance decreasing behaviors are displayed in the presence of a pet or pets.

Social Dominance

See Pack Theory.

Social Hierarchy

See Pack Theory.

Social Learning

Learning by observing and then imitating another being. Ex. Pet A observes Pet B ringing a bell and being let out as a result. Pet A starts ringing the bell to be let out. See imitation.

Social Reinforcers

Social Reinforcers are reinforcers in the form of attention, verbal praise and petting. Social reinforcers need to be delivered with sincerity to be effective.

Splitting and Lumping

See lumping and splitting.

Spontaneous Recovery

The reappearance of a previously extinguished conditioned response or operant behavior.

State Dependent Learning

The mental state of the pet is linked to what she learns. If the pet learns to sit when calm, she will more likely remember this cue when calm, and less likely to remember what "sit" means when in an aroused state.

Stereotypic Behavior

Repetitive behavior that is self-reinforcing. Can be a symptom of Obsessive-Compulsive Disorder which is a medical condition that often requires veterinary pharmaceutical intervention.

Stimulus

Anything a being can perceive that incites action.

Stimulus Control

Using discrimination training we can bring behavior under stimulus control by placing it under the influence of discriminative stimuli. The consequences that follow the operant behavior establish the control exerted by the discrimination stimuli.

A controlling stimulus alters the probability of the operant response. Discriminative stimulus S^D sets the occasion for a high probability response. Another controlling stimulus is S^Δ which sets the occasion for no reinforcement. Both S^D and S^Δ have stimulus control over behavior but their effects are opposite from one another.

Stimulus Generalization

Part of generalization training. The typical generalization that is the goal of most training, that the pet performs the cued behavior in a variety of settings.

Stress

A psychological and physiological state that results from a pet being exposed to a real or perceived environmental stimulus that threatens the pet's ability to meet his needs including safety which results in the pet's inability or greatly decreased ability to learn. Ex. The pet was unable to learn sit because the trash can was blowing in the wind and he was exhibiting fear behaviors while repeatedly glancing at the moving trash can. Stress and fear are huge driving forces of aggression so minimizing stress, pain and fear are critical to aggression prevention.

Successive Approximation

See approximation.

Success Point

The specific criteria that your pet is able to perform successfully. Find your pet's success point and build on it, rather than focusing on what is going wrong.

Success Rate

The rate at which a pet is succeeding while learning a new behavior. Ex. A pet performs the down cue accurately 9/10 attempts this is a 90% success rate. During training sessions trainers should aim for a 90% success rate prior to raising criteria.

Supernormal Stimulus

A stimulus, such as a stuffed life-sized pet, that produces a stronger response than the normal stimulus eliciting that particular response. Can be compared to a sign stimulus which is an ethological term referring to the mechanism that prompts pets to respond to an artificial stimulus as if it was real. An unpublished ASPCA study by Dr. Pam Reid and others showed that pets respond to a stuffed pet that is life size and realistically made as if it was real. The mechanism by which this happens is called a super normal sign stimulus, but in behavior terms it is referred to as stimulus salience. Regardless, the pet biologically responds to what he sees even though the stuffed pet does not smell real. Researchers studying aggression have been using realistic stuffed pets for decades to ethically evaluate aggression in pets.

Superstitious Behavior

The accidental or coincidental reinforcement of behavior that was not intended to be part of the goal behavior or that is now linked with a previously neutral stimulus. Ex. A pet was eating out of his food bowl and a gun shot was fired. Since that event the pet refuses to eat out of his bowl. A pet accidentally spun in a circle before his owner fed him now he always spins in a circle prior to eating.

Systematic Desensitization

To effectively design a systematic desensitization protocol, we need to know the specific conditioned stimulus that elicits the fear, panic or anxiety so we can construct a graded hierarchy starting with levels that elicit attention and not sensitization or potentiation. When planning the graded hierarchy, we need to take into consideration the stimulus variables that could elicit emotional responses such as the distance from the stimulus, the duration of exposure to the stimulus, distractions in the environment, the orientation of the stimulus and any motion or contrast within the stimulus exposure. For each of these variables we will need to develop a stimulus exposure hierarchy.

Sympathetic Nervous System

A part of the autonomic nervous system that mobilizes the pet's energy and resources during times of stress and arousal.

T

Tactile Reinforcement

Using physical touch as a means of reinforcing behavior. According to Bob Bailey tactile reinforcement can be so valuable to some pets that it can be considered a primary reinforcer.

Target Behavior

The goal behavior. The response we are aiming for when training a pet.

Targeting or Target Training

When an object is used for the pet to follow or make contact with. This method of training is an antecedent strategy as it comes before the behavior. The training makes use of a target (stick, mat or other object) as a means of acquiring the end goal behavior.

Task Analysis

The process of developing a written plan of the steps required to teach a new skill.

Terminal Bridge

A terminal bridge marks the end behavior. The pet understands that whatever they are doing when they hear the terminal bridge was exactly correct, stop doing it and get your reinforcement.

Territory

A pet's territory is the sociographical area that the pet may choose to defend. When this area is defended the pet is often labeled territorial.

Three Term Contingency

Another way of expressing the relationship between A →B → C or Antecedent, Behavior and Consequence.

Time-Out

A negative punishment procedure designed to reduce the probability of a target behavior in which access to reinforcement is removed for a particular time period contingent upon the performance of an undesired behavior. Either the pet is removed from the reinforcing environment or the environment is removed from the pet.

There are two common forms of time-out:

1. Pet is removed from the reinforcing environment— you gently take pet and place behind a baby gate or in another room.

2. Owner/reinforcement is removed — the reinforcing contingency is removed from the environment.

Topography

How the behavior looks

Trace Conditioning

One of the four ways conditioning takes place in Respondent Conditioning. In trace conditioning the conditioned stimulus begins and ends before the unconditioned stimulus is presented – the clicker or the verbal "yes". In respondent conditioning the amount of learning depends on the degree to which the conditioned stimulus predicts the unconditioned stimulus. With both trace and delayed conditioning, a conditional response begins to appear after the conditioned stimulus is presented as there is a high degree of CS-US contingency and there is an interstimulus interval.

Transfer Stimulus Control

The mechanism by which a cue is altered. The new cue must be presented first in order for the pet to learn it. New cue, old cue, click and treat. See fading lure

Traumatic Bonding

A strong emotional tie that develops as a result of an abusive relationship which includes an imbalance of power and intermittent exposure to both abuse and affection. Traumatic bonds can be extremely powerful. Ex. Pet that is being beaten but intermittently given affection and lots of reinforcement strongly bonds with abuser, as a result abuser uses bond to falsely justify abuse.

Two-Way Communication

The exchange of information between two beings.

Trial and Error

A term coined by Thorndike. Pets make less errors over repeated trials, they learn from trial and error.

U

Unconditioned Reflex

An unconditioned reflex consists of an unconditioned stimulus (US) and an unconditioned response (UR). An unconditioned stimulus is something that when presented evokes a natural, unconditioned, response, such as blinking when air is pushed towards the eyelid or sweating when stressed or scared. Freeze dried liver offered to a dog is an example of a US and the dog drooling is an example of the resulting UR.

Unconditioned Reinforcers

Unconditioned reinforcers are innately reinforcing. They are called primary reinforcers as they are not dependent on an association with another reinforcer.

Unconditioned Stimulus

A term used in Respondent Conditioning. An unconditioned stimulus is something that when presented evokes a natural, unconditioned response, such as blinking when air is pushed towards the eyelid or sweating when stressed or scared.

V

Variable Reinforcement

See Schedules of reinforcement.

Vicarious Reinforcement

This term means the reinforcement resulting from observing another pet being reinforced for a behavior. Often used or attributed to modeling.

Variability

The differences in behavior being offered. Often seen in shaping when reinforcement is withheld for a previously reinforced criterion and extinction begins. This gives the trainer an opportunity to reinforce the next criteria they deem appropriate.

Variable Schedule of Reinforcement

See Reinforcement schedules

Visual Prompt

A cue that is designed for the pet to see

Voluntary Behavior

Responses that are under the pet's conscious control and are thus more likely to be modified by operant conditioning. Ex. dog sits politely for petting. An example of involuntary behavior is drooling.

W

X

Y

Yerkes –Dodson Law

In psychology an important law that states that motivation occurs on a bell curve. Too much deprivation causes poor performance and likewise not enough deprivation causes poor performance. The same applies to satiation. Some trainers may attribute lack of performance to not enough deprivation, not realizing that too much deprivation will have a negative impact on learning. This is law relates to sport psychology and is why peak performances are called "zone" experiences.

Yippee Effect

This is a Dog trainer slang term for the outcome of ideal behavior modification when the previously feared or stress inducing stimulus elicits a new conditioned emotional response of joy.

Z

The Contributors

Niki Tudge - M.B.A, PCBC-A, CDBC, CDT

Niki is the Founder of The Pet Professional Guild, DogNostics Career Center, The DogSmith and the President of Doggone safe. Niki has combined her "people" teaching and pet training skills with her commitment to pet rescue and substantial business knowledge to create a proprietary system of education known as ARRF® supported by an operational implementation process called MTR®. Niki is equipped with a unique combination of business experience, pet training and pet behavior expertise, a background in exceptional customer service, certification as a trainer of trainers and many years consulting to pet rescue groups.

Louise Stapleton-Frappell - B.A. Hons, PCT- A, PCBC-A, CAP[3], CTDI, DN-FSG, DN-CPCT, CWRI

Louise is a Partner and Faculty Member of DogNostics Career Center and Board Member of The Pet Professional Guild. Louise has constantly built on her knowledge and furthered her education in the field of force-free, rewards based, science-based pet training. The creator of the DogNostics' Dog Trainer Certification Program, Louise has presented at conferences internationally and has gained a reputation for expertly teaching and training humans and canines at her own establishment, The DogSmith of Estepona, in Southern Spain, where she offers a wide range of both group and private classes and pet dog services.

Angelica Steinker, M. Ed, PCBC-A, CDBT, CDBC, CAP[2]

Angelica owns Courteous Canine, Inc. DogSmith of Tampa. Specializing in dog aggression, she is a Companion Pet Sciences graduate and former faculty. She is currently a faculty member of DogNostics Career Center. She has presented for The Pet Professional Guild in England and in Brazil. She has been published in the Journal of Veterinary Behavior and has written two books. Angelica is passionate about emotional learning and would love to continue to bring this overlooked and under-allocated learning process to the dog behavior world. She also enjoys bringing positive psychology to behavior consulting, which ensures that the dog and owner's emotional states are improved as a result of behavior change.

CPSIA information can be obtained
at www.ICGtesting.com
Printed in the USA
BVHW081058110820
586103BV00015B/405

9 780692 186695